Treasure in the Multiplication Maze

Treasure in the Multiplication Maze

Learn the Times Tables through a Hilarious & Adventurous Hunt

C.V. Jayagovind

White Falcon Publishing

Treasure in the Multiplication Maze
C.V. Jayagovind

Published by White Falcon Publishing
Chandigarh, India

First Edition, 2024

Cover design by White Falcon Publishing, 2024
Cover image source freepik.com

ISBN - 978-93-341-4756-8

About the Book

Humans have been printing the Times Tables since time immemorial. It is not difficult to imagine the Neanderthal child, after a long day on the back of her hunting parents, yearning to reach the cave to grab her Times Tables. **LOL!** Human life improved a lot from then through the inventions of fire, the wheel, the light bulb, the steam engine, television, the internet, **pizza**, **doughnuts**, and **ONLINE GAMES**! But one thing has not changed - the 21st-century child reads THE SAME OLD TIMES TABLES, trying to memorize them somehow.

No doubt, it is important to know the tables like the back of your hand. There is no 'right age' **WRITTEN IN STONE** to learn the tables, and it may vary from one child to another. But what we know with certainty is that every child has the ability and memory to learn them. What is required is a path that avoids the associated fear and boredom, tools that break them into bits and pieces for memory retention, and finally, some effort to practice them to perfection.

Imagine an *adventurous and fun-filled river rafting ride* where you also get to pick up a few drifting bottles with useful secrets at every turn. This book offers the same by taking you through a nail-biting and rib-tickling adventure of three kids in their school. As you race against time with them in their curious chase, you also get to see how easy the times tables are with a few **never-before-seen** and *fun-to-learn* tips and tricks.

Once you grasp those pointers, you can play the games at the end of this book. They can be played with a pair of dice or a pack of cards with friends and family or by oneself. You will end up practicing the tables and **becoming a pro!**

Go ahead, get on the fun ride.

To all the parents
who want their kids to
achieve their full potential

Table of Contents

About the Book v

Chapter 1 Lightning at lunch break 1

Chapter 2 The soup-er surprise 10

Chapter 3 Pepper-on-pizza 22

Chapter 4 Clues from the blues 35

Chapter 5 Dany, the dude 46

Chapter 6 The fight with the class leader....... 67

Chapter 7 Oh, my gosh! 82

Chapter 8 1942... how it all began 94

Square of all numbers 106

Times Table Grid 107

Times Tables Games 108

Acknowledgment 114

About the Author-cum-Illustrator 115

CHAPTER 1

Lightning at lunch break

"Nine times five?" Mrs. Rodriguez repeated the question to Aria.

The entire class was silent. Everyone, except Jay, was looking down to avoid eye contact, hoping that Mrs. Rodriguez would not call their name. After all, 'prevention is better than cure.'

And no! Jay was not looking at Mrs. Rodriguez, wanting to answer. In fact, he had not even heard the question. Like always, he was looking out of the window of their first-floor classroom at those playing on the basketball court.

"Okay, Aria and the entire class. I will give you one more week. Please learn all the multiplication tables by next Monday," said Mrs. Rodriguez, the Math teacher.

There was a sigh of relief from the whole class - no more tests would be asked this week. Aria looked around and smiled at her best friends, Kai and Nevan, sitting to her right. They called themselves 'The Talented Three' and shared the same seat row in the class and school bus in one of the best combined schools in the city.

Mrs. Rodriguez continued, "All of you must learn the multiplication tables in this grade. Times tables are for Math like..."

"Breathing is for living," Nevan and Kai said together in a low voice, having heard it many times.

"Jinx!"

"Double jinx!"

"Yes, Nevan. Do you want to say something to the class?" Mrs. Rodriguez had heard Nevan's loud voice, trying to speak before Kai.

"No," replied Nevan with a 'Why are you asking me that?' face.

"Okay. Tanya, help me distribute these flyers," Mrs. Rodriguez called the Class Leader. "Children, here is the flyer announcing the Math Olympiad Test for this year. I would like all the students of this class to participate."

A piece of paper fell out from between the flyers. Tanya handed it to Mrs. Rodriguez, who looked at it.

"An old piece of paper with some numbers," said Mrs. Rodriguez, examining it.

"What numbers?" asked Adrian, the nerd of the class, sitting in the first row.

"Not sure. The flyers were kept in a basement cupboard that was unused for a long time. Tanya, pin it to the sideboard. Let everyone have a look to see if it makes any sense."

TRRRRRNGGGGG! The bell rang for the much-awaited long break.

As the silent class erupted into chatting and yelling sounds, Aria started reading her Olympiad flyer. She did not want to register last year, and her dad agreed with the condition that she would have to participate in the next year.

"Dads and moms have a way of getting you to agree to their conditions at the right moment, don't they?" thought Aria.

MODE OF EXAM: ONLINE

"Come on! Why can't it be held in some other school like it used to be earlier? It would be fun visiting a different school and planting some pranks in their classroom," said Aria, turning to Kai, who was beside her. Was – because that was 10 seconds back. Now, Aria saw Kai standing in front of the sideboard, observing the piece of paper pinned on it.

Aria opened her folder, turned the flyer upside down, and slid it in. She always kept the flyers she disliked with the blank side up so that she was not reminded of them constantly.

She walked up to Kai and looked at the pinned-up paper herself.

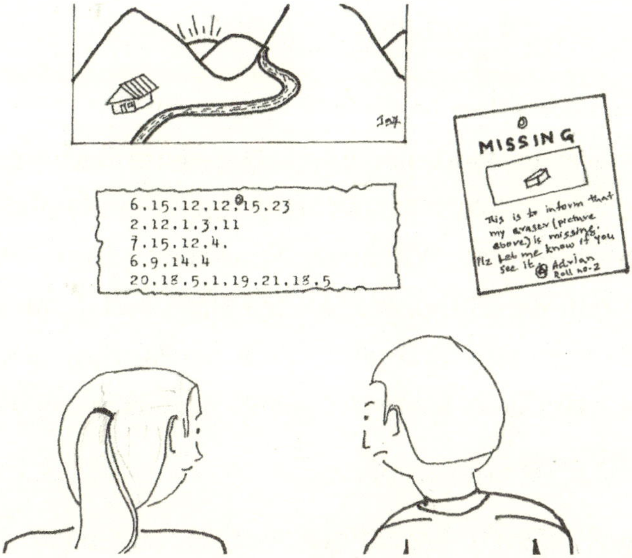

6,15,12,12,15,23-2,12,1,3,11-7,15,12,4,--6,9,14,4-20,18,5,1,19,21,18,5

"Kai, what on earth is this?"

Kai had watched all episodes of the latest children's detective series. Not just once, but twice. He had since developed an investigator's mind.

"Hmm. It is typed on an old-style typewriter. And the paper looks very old."

Nevan, who came back from the bathroom, also started looking.

"Argh, these numbers!" said Aria.

Aria referred to Math as a 'necessary evil', a term she learned from her mom. Her mom had a rule that allowed Aria to use her mom's mobile phone only once a day. Whenever Aria asked, "How come you can use the phone all the time, but I can't?" Her mom would reply, "It's a necessary evil for me, Ari. I have to do my posts regularly; they will be waiting."

'They' refers to her followers on social media.

She posted healthy and nutritional dishes and recipes on her social media page 'Nutri_Ninjas_6'.

This not only robbed Aria of her mobile gaming time but also earned her nasty looks from many classmates at lunchtime. Nutri_Ninjas_6's tagline said it all, "Health Before Taste." Some of her classmates' moms followed Nutri_Ninjas_6 and prepared some of those not-so-tasty-but-healthy dishes for school meals.

"The numbers don't seem to be in any particular order. See, some numbers are repeating as well," observed Kai, examining the old piece of paper.

"And the highest number is 23," said Nevan, a regular at the Math Olympiad.

"I feel like this is a secret message. 6, 15, 12, 12... Which is the 6th alphabet?" asked Detective Kai.

"F," replied Aria instantly. "15th is O, then L, L, O," read Aria. Now, Aria was interested. She loved English and was an avid reader. The school librarian had once 'appreciated' her that even the real witches wouldn't have read so many books on magic and witchcraft as Aria had.

"And the 23rd alphabet is W. FOLLOW!" Aria read the first word.

"Bro, THIS IS CRAZY," shouted Nevan.

"Shush. Let's note down the numbers and go to our seat," Kai knew how to handle such secret stuff.

During the lunch break, the class was noisier than the food court at the downtown mall. Some were swallowing their meals; some were distributing their 'Nutri_Ninjas_6 food' to their neighbors so that they could show an empty meal box at home. In the middle of all the chaos, three children had not opened their meal boxes. Aria, Kai, and Nevan sat shocked and still as if they were struck by lightning. Kai's Rough Notebook was open on the table, with the numbers decoded.

Follow black gold, find treasure.

Kai slowly pulled down his notebook from the table to his lap. He looked around to see if anyone was watching him or the notebook. Everyone was busy eating, talking, and shouting.

Jay was still looking out of the window.

CHAPTER 2

The soup-er surprise

"Let's inform Mrs. Rodriguez," whispered Aria to Nevan as she opened the lunchbox.

"What if she takes this as some silly joke?" asked Nevan in his usual loud voice.

"Hey, what's the joke, old man? Tell me," said a voice from behind Nevan.

Nevan was shocked and turned around. It was Sasha who sat behind him. Her mouth was bulging with whatever she was eating. Nevan called her Snoopy Sasha as she was always curious to overhear others. Sasha called Nevan 'Old man', since he wore round glasses and spoke loudly, similar to Sasha's Grandpa.

Nevan thought for a second and said in a serious tone, "Did you hear? Aliens are landing on Earth tomorrow."

He looked at Kai from the corner of his eye. Kai's mouth opened as if he took Nevan's words seriously. Sasha wasn't interested in hearing more.

"Okay, let's go and meet Mrs. Rodriguez as soon as I finish my pasta. I can't miss my pasta," whispered Nevan to Aria.

TRRRRRNGGGGG! The break was over.

Nevan looked at his pasta like a hungry lion inside a cage, watching a gazelle walk past outside. He closed the meal box.

"Guys, guys, I've heard from my grandpa that our school was a safe house during World War Two," whispered Kai to Nevan and Aria as he took the seat between them on the school bus. They couldn't talk after the break, and now it was time for them to take the school bus back home.

Aria had never understood why Kai called out 'Guys' twice whenever he was excited. Even if it was to talk about encountering a T-Rex, wasn't 'Guys' by itself plural?

But Aria had no time to ask about that now.

"World War Two? When was that?" exclaimed Aria.

"After World War I," said Nevan seriously.

"I know that. I just meant it's been a long time," explained Aria.

"Listen, guys... Grandpa had also mentioned that many rich families hid their money and jewelry during the war, out of fear of getting looted," continued Kai.

The bus started moving.

"What if some rich guy hid his things in our school and left that note as a clue for his family?" whispered Kai.

"THERE IS A TREASURE IN OUR SCHOOL?!" exclaimed Nevan excitedly in his typical, loud voice.

"Excuse me, a treasure in our school?" said a voice from behind.

Nevan turned around with a frozen face. It was Snoopy Sasha again! In the seat right behind him, again. And her mouth was still bulged.

Aria was sure that the secret was out this time. She looked at Kai with a frowning face.

"So, this was the big silly joke you made up during the break, meh," said Sasha, continuing to chew her bus snacks and chat with her friend in the next seat.

The three were relieved. Aria leaned forward so that Sasha couldn't hear and said, "This is what they say – Behind every successful boy, there is always a stupid girl," and laughed.

The 7th-grade boy sitting in front of Aria turned back upon hearing this and gave a strange smile.

"Now, why is he smiling?" thought Aria.

Kai got off the bus one stop early to talk with Aria and Nevan, who were neighbors.

"So, what do you think of this?" asked Nevan.

"I think that whoever this rich guy was, he and his family were math teachers," said Kai.

“Maybe. But how to follow the Black Gold?” asked Nevan.

“Follow means Find. We need to find Black Gold,” explained Aria, drawing from her experience in horror and adventure books.

“What is Black Gold? I haven’t seen or heard of such a thing,” said Nevan.

“I’ll try to search it on Dad’s phone today. Now, let me run home quickly,” said Kai.

“Okay. Send a message to our group if you find it. I also have to go. Mom has told me not to hang around much after getting off the bus,” said Aria.

“Even my dad has told me that. He is worried about those crazy guys in the ninth grade,” said Kai.

“Oh. It’s the opposite for me,” said Aria.

“You mean your mom is worried about the crazy girls in the ninth grade?” asked Nevan.

"No. My mom fears I will drive someone crazy if I stay long," smiled Aria.

It was late in the evening when Nevan opened his English books to do the homework. On the Contents page of the textbook, his eyes fell upon Chapter 9: Treasure Island.

"OH, MY GOODNESS!" Nevan exclaimed.

"What happened?" asked his mom, who had just picked up her phone to browse. "Don't tell me that all the words in your English book have magically vanished."

"No, Mom. I must check my messages; there is something important," said Nevan.

"Come on, Nevan. This is what you do every time you open your English book."

"No, no, this is urgent. JUST ONE MINUTE."

"I have to send a few messages. I'll be late for cooking if you take the phone now. Will you help me with the soup?" asked his mom.

"Okay, okay. Yes," Nevan was used to getting chores in exchange for using electronic devices. He always wondered who would ask these parents to do chores after their long hours on laptops and mobile phones.

He opened the "Talented Three" group.

Nevan's Friend Kai's Dad: Found it, guys. It's oil!

Aria's Mom: Oil? What? 😮

Nevan's Friend Kai's Dad: Black Gold, Google says it's oil...*petrolium.*

Aria's Mom: It's *PETROLEUM, and not PETROLIUM*

Nevan's Friend Kai's Dad: Ya whatever 🤷

Aria's Mom: Where can we find petroleum in the school? 🧐

Nevan's Friend Kai's Dad: Maybe on the school buses 🤔

Aria's Mom: Does it mean we should follow the school buses? 🚌 🚌

Nevan's Friend Kai's Dad: idk

Aria's Mom: What's idk?

Nevan's Friend Kai's Dad: I don't know

Aria's Mom: Then why did you type that?

"Come on, @Aria's Mom, 'idk' stands for 'I Don't Know,'" typed Nevan.

"Which bus should we follow? The school has a lot of buses," he asked.

"Okay, Nevan, JUST ONE MINUTE over," called out his mom.

"Yup, giving in a moment," said Nevan.

"Come, let's get the dinner ready. I'm so hungry that I could eat a horse," said his mom, pulling the phone out of his hand.

"Oh, a horse will taste awful," said Nevan, not happy with the phone being taken away.

She looked at Nevan and said, “It will be better than all the junk food you ate over the weekend.”

“Is it even legal to eat a horse?” Nevan asked seriously.

“I’m sure the judge will pardon me if he can feel how hungry I am,” said his mom.

Nevan washed the soup bowls and slowly filled them up with the ladle.

“Good job, Nevan,” commented his mom.

“Thank you,” he said as he was already out of the kitchen.

"Hey, you've forgotten to add something," called Mom.

"What?"

"Think."

"Oh no, not the healthy protein powder you made."

"Aha, now that you remember, add that as well."

"What else?" Nevan did not want to guess more and get into 'more trouble.'

"Black Gold!" said Mom.

His mouth widened.

"What?"

"Black Gold."

He regained his senses and asked, "Oil?"

"No, dear. Pepper,"

"Oh, pepper? Is it called Black Gold?"

"Yes, black pepper was very costly in ancient times, and kingdoms used to pay in gold to obtain it from India."

"Ahem, that's very interesting. Thanks for the info," he was excited now.

"Welcome, dear. Don't forget to add the pepper. And yes, the protein powder."

CHAPTER 3

Pepper-on-pizza

"Yes, that's also correct. I checked on Google after seeing your message last night," said Kai as soon as he saw Nevan and Aria on the bus the next morning.

"So, what should we find...oil or pepper?" asked Aria.

"For oil, we don't know which bus to follow," said Kai.

"And pepper will be available only in one place in the whole school," said Nevan, looking at Kai and Aria.

"Kitchen. The cafeteria kitchen," Aria sounded excited.

"Okay, let's check out the cafeteria during the lunch break," said Kai.

"The lunch break? I don't want to miss my pasta today, ALSO," frowned Nevan.

"Come on, you get pasta EVERY DAY. Even if you don't want a break, the pasta needs one," joked Aria.

"I am happy to skip my sandwiches topped with some NutriNinja6's protein powder," said Kai.

Aria gave a nasty look to Kai, knowing that he was pulling her leg about her mom's recipe channel.

The period before the lunch break was supposed to be Math. However, the Social Studies teacher, Mr. Davidson, came in to inform that Mrs. Rodriguez was on leave for the day and had asked the class to study the multiplication tables and write them down on a sheet of paper. He asked the Class Leader, Tanya, to manage the class discipline.

Aria immediately pulled out the 'Order of the Witches' book from the bag and buried her head in it. Nevan started writing the tables.

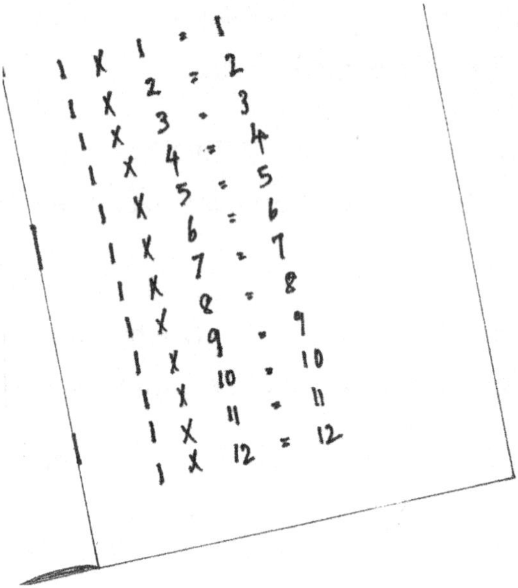

As he finished the table of 1, his tummy reminded him of the pasta waiting in his lunch box. He looked at the big clock in the class.

“Bro, shall we check the cafeteria now? We have forty-five minutes free,” said Nevan to Kai.

“How? Tanya is watching the class,” said Kai.

“Mr. Davidson didn’t say that we cannot walk out,” observed Nevan.

“That’s also correct. But what do we tell Tanya?” asked Kai.

“Aria, how can we get out?” asked Nevan, straining to keep his voice low.

“If I had brought my magic wand, I could have made her doze off or fly away,” Aria was still in the magical world.

“Do you REALLY have a wand?”

“You know, the one I made by folding up old newspaper and then painting it,” Aria said with a smile.

“Kai, can you ask Tanya? You both were in the same class last year,” Nevan turned to Kai.

“No chance,” said Kai. “She thinks I didn’t vote for her in the Class Leader election.”

“Did you vote for her?” asked Nevan.

“Of course... No!”

“Oh Bro, I voted for her. But how will she know that? They should publish who all voted for the winning candidate. Else what is the use of voting for them?” asked Nevan.

“What!” exclaimed Kai.

“Hey, I am going to the bathroom. Why don’t you guys also come out giving the same excuse?” suggested Aria.

“Yes, I actually want to go to the bathroom,” said Kai.

The boys’ bathroom had toilet rooms on both sides leading up to the urinals.

As Kai was relieving himself, Nevan spoke in his usual voice.

“You know how I fooled Leo, who was my class leader last year? He wouldn’t allow anyone to go to the bathroom during free periods, and I wanted to go once. I went to him with a fearful face and told him that there was a big dam that was going to explode if not opened.”

“And then?” Kai asked laughingly.

“He asked me, ‘So what?’“ continued Nevan. “I replied that I own that dam and only I can open it. I just walked out of the class as he was still figuring out what I said."

Kai was back, standing beside Nevan, and both laughed.

The door of the restroom on their right opened, and Leo emerged, staring at Nevan.

"That dam almost leaked when the class teacher called you after I reported to her. Remember?" Leo shrugged and walked away.

Not wanting to face Leo, Nevan looked the other way.

"STRANGE! These toilets have been numbered 1, 3, 5, 7... Where are the other numbers?" Nevan wondered aloud.

"Look this side!" said Kai.

"Oh, okay, here they are: 2, 4, 6..." Nevan observed on the opposite side.

"Why can't they write in order?" wondered Kai.

"Odd numbers on one side and even on the other. Actually, the numbers on the even side look like the table of 2!" said Nevan.

"Oh, is it? Let me check. Two ones are two, two twos are four...," Kai started verifying.

Nevan walked ahead and finished reading it, "Two twelves are Twenty-Four. It's easy. It's all the even numbers and they go 2, 4, 6, 8 and then become two digits but still end with 0, 2, 4, 6, 8."

"Wow. I can say the tables just like that... 2, 4, 6, 8, 10, 12, 14, 16, 18, 20, 22, 24," said Kai.

"Yes, that's counting by twos, instead of the regular counting by ones."

"See, Mr. Davidson asked us to sit and learn the tables. But we are studying them when we came out," Kai giggled.

"True. But we have to write them down also," remembered Nevan.

Kai looked around and found a roll of toilet paper. He tore off a piece from it and pulled out the pen from his pocket.

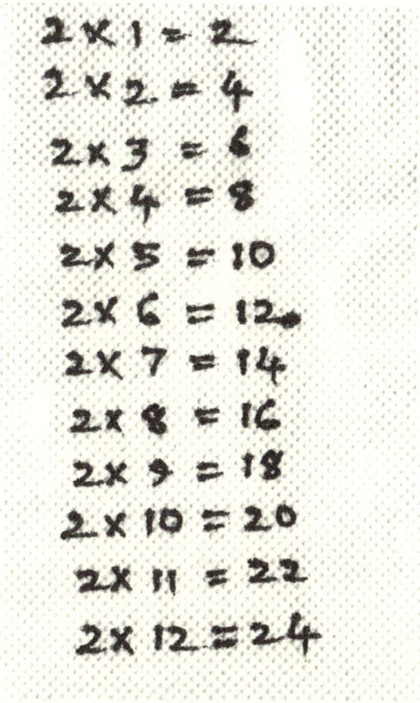

As they entered the cafeteria, the scent of fresh pizza filled the air.

“Shall we get some pizza? I have some money in my pocket,” Nevan asked.

“Not a bad idea,” Aria couldn’t resist either.

“How about we eat one piece each quickly?” asked Nevan.

“You don’t get three pieces. There are 4 pieces in the smallest size,” said Kai.

“Okay, I can manage the extra piece,” Nevan said with a smile.

As they ordered and sat down, Nevan said, “Maybe we could have ordered the medium size. We would have gotten 6 pieces, 2 for each of the 3 of us.”

“Come on, Nevan, your pasta is also waiting in your lunchbox,” reminded Aria.

“I know, that’s why I said 2 pieces each. Otherwise, I would have loved to have 3 pieces.”

“No, we can’t get 9 pieces. There are only 8 pieces in the large size,” said Aria.

“Then we could have gotten 2 medium ones. Total 12 pieces, 4 for each,” said Kai, laughing.

“See this, since there are 3 of us, we want the number of pieces to be like the table of 3. It’s 3, 6, 9, or 12...” found Nevan.

“Or 3 fives are 15, 3 sixes are 18,” continued Kai.

“This is what Mrs. Rodriguez said: that multiplication is repeated addition, right? Each number is obtained by adding 3 to the previous one,” observed Aria.

“Yes. 3 x 5 is nothing but getting 3 pizza pieces five times. So, adding 3 five times, like 3 + 3 + 3 + 3 + 3, is the same as 3 x 5, which is 15,” said Nevan.

“Let’s write it down. It sounds like an easy one, like 2,” said Kai, taking the cafeteria bill to write.”

“If we want an odd number of pieces per person, the total number of pieces required is also odd. If we want an even number, the total is also even,” observed Aria as Kai was writing.

“3 elevens are 33, 3 twelves are 36,” Kai finished writing.

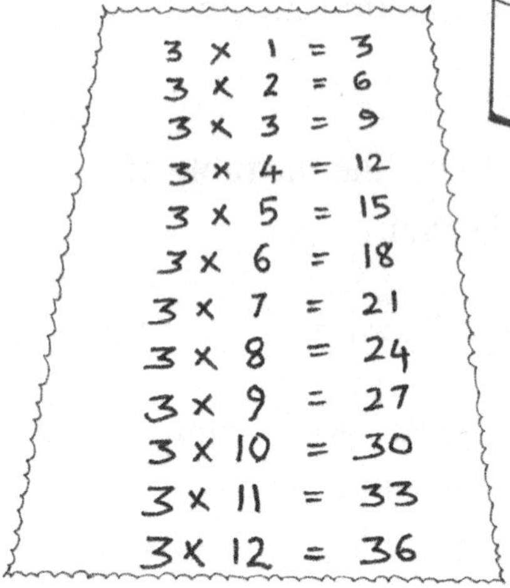

The pizza was ready, and Nevan picked it up.

“Wow. It’s heaven,” Nevan pounced onto it.

“It’s a very spicy heaven. A lot of pepper on it,” said Aria.

“Guys, pepper! We need to find where the pepper is kept in the kitchen,” Kai stood up.

“Yes, yes. But let’s finish this,” Nevan didn’t move.

“Nevan, imagine if we find the treasure and you can buy pizzas every day with the money...,” Aria said dramatically.

Nevan swallowed his next piece and stood up.

They sneaked into the kitchen and bumped into the Cafeteria Chef.

“Hi, Chef. We loved the pizza; it was deliciously spicy. Can I see which black pepper you use so that I can ask my mom to get the same one?” asked Aria.

“Thank you, kids. It’s the regular pepper, in the regular place. See the spice rack over here,” said the chef, walking towards the other side of the kitchen.

Kai was quick to search the spice rack.

"I don't see enough space for treasure here," whispered Aria.

Kai's eyes caught something at the far corner of the spice rack.

"Kids, do you want to smell the pepper?" the chef asked, standing right behind them.

"Err, no. I got it," said Aria.

They quickly walked out of the cafeteria. Kai pulled out the piece of paper he had pocketed.

CHAPTER 4

Clues from the blues

"Let me read the message this time," Aria snatched the paper from Kai, hoping to announce the alphabets based on the numbers. But it wasn't as easy as she thought.

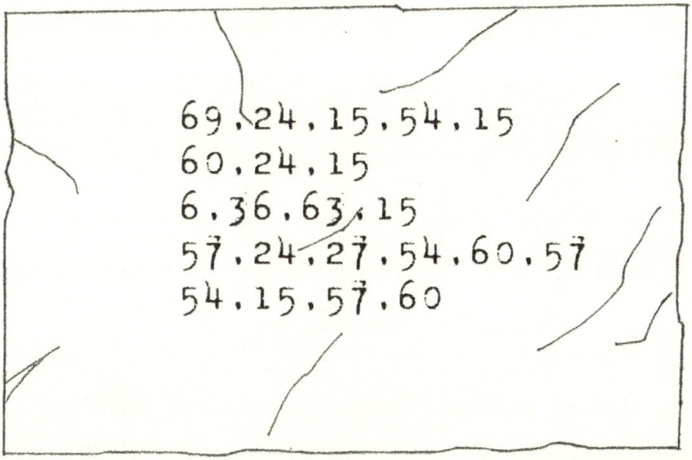

She looked at it for a few seconds and gave it to Kai. "Okay, you found it. You read."

Nevan peeked in.

"Okay, the number to alphabet code doesn't seem to be working. 69, 24, 15... There is no 69th alphabet," announced Nevan.

"Of course," said Aria.

"Yes. But I remember writing some of these numbers recently. 24 is 2 x 12 and also 3 x 8," said Kai.

"And 15 is 3 x 5... 6 is 3 x 2, 36 is 3 x 12," observed Nevan.

"So, are these numbers from the table of 3?" asked Aria.

"Looks so. 69 is...let's see. 3 x 10 is 30, and so, 3 x 20 is twice of 30, that means 60. Then 63, 66, 69...So, 69 is 3 x 23," said Nevan.

Kai took a napkin from the nearby table and started writing the numbers being multiplied by 3. 24 is 3 x 8, so write 8 next. 15 is 3 x 5, so 5.

23, 8, 5, 18, 5 - 20, 8, 5 – 2, 12, 21, 5 – 19, 8, 9, 18, 20, 19 – 18, 5, 19, 20

"And, the 23rd alphabet is W. 8th alphabet is H," said Aria.

"E, R, E, T," Aria was quick to spell the alphabets.

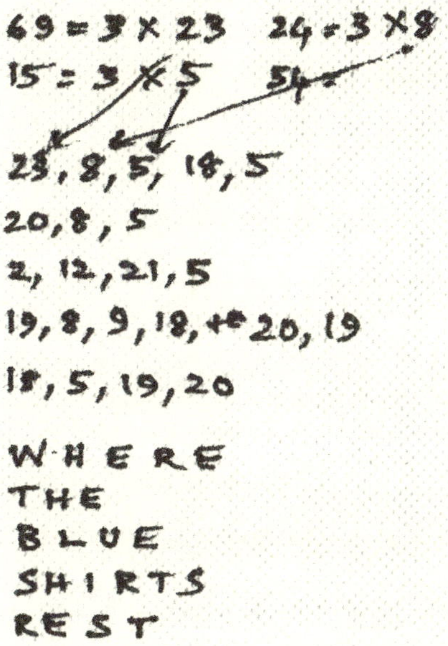

"Blue shirts? Where are the blue shirts in the school?"

"Shirts are always in cupboards and closets," said Aria.

"Or on people when they wear it," said Kai, looking around.

A school bus driver in a blue shirt was walking towards the cafeteria.

"The Drivers' Amenity Centre! Where the blue shirts rest," said Kai.

"Brilliant! Let's hurry. Hope we find the treasure there," said Nevan.

They had to cross the school grounds to reach the Bus Parking Area where the Drivers' Amenity Center was located. A few students were playing 'Take the Flag' on the grounds. Aria ran ahead quickly, with Kai and Nevan following.

They heard two long whistles and stopped to look around. The Physical Education Instructor, Mr. Watson, walked up to Aria.

"Hey, Aria. It's good that I saw you. We have a meeting of the Apollo House tomorrow during the second short break. Your House Captain is on leave. Can you inform and show this announcement to the other House members in your class?" he asked, handing over the flyer.

“But I don’t know who all the House members are,” said Aria, trying to catch her breath.

Kai and Nevan had caught up.

“Hey, we’ve made it easy this year. What is your class roll number?” asked Mr. Watson.

“Four,”

“Cool. We’ve just placed students sequentially, one by one, into each of the 4 houses and then repeated the same order. So, if you are number 4, the next member in Apollo House will be roll number 8, then 12, and so on,” he explained.

"Okay. 4 x 1 = 4, 4 x 2 = 8, 4 x 3 = 12..." stopped Aria.

"4 x 4 = 16, 4 x 5 = 20..." continued Nevan.

"Yes. Numbers ending in 4, 8, 2, 6, 0, and then again ending in the same order 24, 28, 32, 36, and 40," said Mr. Watson.

"Oh, my God! That is so cool – 4,8,2,6,0. I will put this trick on my video channel," announced Aria.

"Oh, you have a channel? What's the name? Let me check it out," asked Mr. Watson.

"Uhm, it's called Amazing Aria. But I don't have many subscribers, as of now," said Aria shyly.

"That's alright. Vloggers with a million subscribers actually buy subscribers and likes. A few thousand subscribers are good enough," said Mr. Watson.

"Actually... um... I have three, as of now. My dad, mom, and the girl next door."

"Oh, okay. No worries. You have one subscriber outside the family to start with," he tried to sound supportive.

"You can build more from here. You know – Nothing is impossible, even the word 'impossible' says 'I'm possible,'" he continued.

"Yes, sir. But is 'I'm possible' even correct grammatically?" Aria responded.

Mr. Watson stared at her for a second and then walked away.

"Ah, I didn't tell him that my neighbor subscribed only after making me subscribe to her channel," said Aria.

Nevan looked at Kai. Kai took out his pen and pulled the flyer from Aria's hand to write the table of 4.

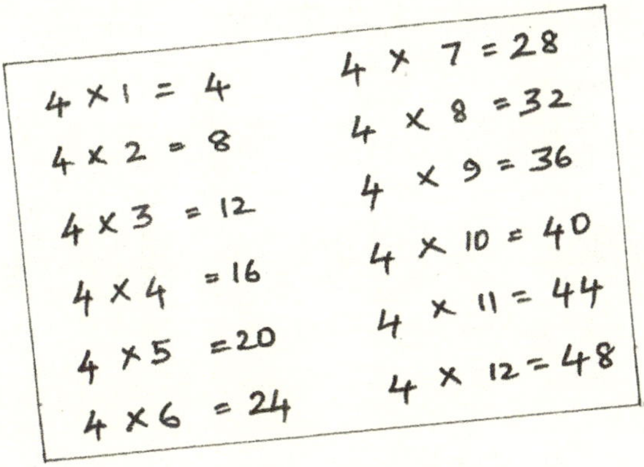

The drivers looked curiously when they saw the three students walking into the Amenity Center. As they entered, there was an old metallic board of 'Waiting Area' with an arrow pointing downward. They walked down the staircase into the basement.

"Yes, kids, how can we help you?" asked a tall, muscular man with a rough voice.

"Are the enemies bombing the place?" asked another driver.

"BOMBING! Who? Why?" Nevan was a little frightened.

"Nothing, kids. We keep joking that our place is like a bomb-safe bunker."

"Hmm. So, was this a safe bunker during World War Two?" Kai became interested.

"World War? When was that? Sorry, kids, we were not around at that time," said the muscular man, and everyone laughed.

"Maybe this bunker was where the rich math guy hid the treasure," whispered Kai to Aria.

"Hey, I know you. Aren't you on bus number seven? I drive you folks to and fro," said Mr. Stewart, who walked in.

"Yes. You pick us up first in the morning and drop us back last in the afternoon," said Aria, with the word 'last' elongated to emphasize it.

"Yes, kids, that's how the route goes. Sorry."

"That's alright. We like being on the bus for a long time; we get to talk more," said Aria.

"Haha, that's good. But both are the same for me, you know. It takes the same distance if I take the morning route or the exact opposite route in the afternoon," said Mr. Stewart.

"Aha! It's like 2 x 3 = 6 and 3 x 2 = 6, isn't it?" Nevan was quick to say that.

"Hmmm...yeah, right," agreed Mr. Stewart.

"Yes, whichever number you put first, two numbers give the same product," Nevan explained.

"Product? Which product are we talking about?" Mr. Stewart was confused.

"Whenever we multiply numbers, the result we obtain is called the product of the numbers being multiplied," answered Nevan.

"You are good with your math, boy," said Mr. Stewart.

"Thank you," said Nevan, smiling, happy with the appreciation he received.

"But you are very mischievous on the bus, you know? Remember, I had warned you three times for walking inside the moving bus."

That took the proud smile off Nevan's face.

"Um, sorry for that," said Nevan.

"That's alright, boy. No one is perfect, that's why pencils have erasers, you know?" said Mr. Stewart, smiling at Nevan and Aria.

"But we will start using pens from next year. What do we do then? Will we have to be perfect?" asked Aria.

Mr. Stewart was no longer smiling.

While this conversation was happening, Kai had slipped off to search the rusty lockers behind the seats.

"Guys, I think we can go now," said Kai with a slight smile.

"Oh, is the World War over now? Thank you for visiting our little bunker," said the tall man, smiling.

"Goodbye," said Mr. Stewart, relieved that he didn't have to explain whether those using pens must be perfect or not.

CHAPTER 5

Dany, the dude

"So, they didn't hide the treasure in the bunker either," Aria said disappointedly, once they came out of the Drivers' Amenities Center.

"And they thought changing the codes would make it difficult for some random guys to find it," said Kai, looking at the dusty piece of paper he found in the rustiest locker in the drivers' waiting room.

28,60
76,20,20
4,56
4,52,60,20,8,4

In a few seconds, Nevan's eyes started to shine.

"But they sure didn't expect that the Talented Three would lay their hands on these codes. It's... the... TABLE OF 4. They have used the table of 4 to code this message. 28 is 4 X 7, so 7, 7th alphabet," said Nevan, turning to Aria.

"G," said Aria.

"60 is 40 + 20, so 4 x 10 + 4 x 5, 4 x 15, so next is the 15th alphabet."

Nevan announced the numbers one by one.

"19,5,5, space, 1,14, space, 1,13,15,5,2,1."

With each number, Aria unemotionally gave out the corresponding alphabet, like a Spelling Bee contestant spelling out the complicated words. Kai wrote down each alphabet.

GO SEE AN AMOEBA

"What? Did we make a mistake?" Kai wondered

"Is 'An Amoeba' some new movie or series?" asked Aria.

"No, Bro, Amoeba is that small thingy, that small animal or whatever," Nevan remembered from the Children's Encyclopedia his dad had got for him.

"What? Like ants?" asked Kai.

"No, it's very small, tiny. It's like bacteria, we can't see normally," explained Nevan.

"Oh my gosh, germs! Then how do we see one?" Aria clicked her tongue and looked into her palms, hoping to see those germs that her mom said always existed on everyone's hands.

"Maybe we need one of those thingies, what do you call that – a telescope?" said Nevan.

"A telescope is for seeing stars and planets. Ah, isn't it a microscope? I've read about it," said Aria.

"Yes! But where do we get a microscope now to see an amoeba?" asked Nevan.

"And for what? Is the next set of wacky numbers written on some amoeba!?" frowned Aria.

"Hey, aren't such items used in science experiments? Did they mean the Science Lab where the high schoolers go?" Kai found out how it could be linked to the school.

"Okay, that sounds possible. Let's check out the lab."

"But we need to hurry now. I think half of the Math period is over by now," warned Nevan, with the image of pasta flashing in his mind.

"Okay, the labs are in The Annexe, on the back side of the Main building. We can take a shortcut through the Amphitheater over there to the back side," Kai pointed out and started running.

“Hey, it’s the TABLE OF 5!”

The three stopped running right in the middle of the Amphitheatre upon hearing this. They looked at each other, and the same thought ran through Aria, Kai, and Nevan’s minds. Was someone else chasing the treasure? Did someone get their hands on the next clue before them?

They turned around to see Ms. Lin, the Dance Teacher, standing on the stage with some students from the school dance team.

“Yes, it’s easy to schedule the programs if each program is for five minutes,” Ms. Lin said.

“So, the first dance is at 11 AM. The next at 11:05 AM, then 11:10, 11:15, 11:20... Just keep writing the table of 5 after 11,” said one of the student dancers, who appeared to be the lead dancer of the group.

“Looks like they are scheduling the program for the Dance Festival planned for next month,” whispered Kai to Nevan and Aria as they walked towards the stage.

"But how do you know to find the table of 5 so quickly?" Aria boldly asked the group.

Everyone turned around.

"Err...we are just learning the tables. Can you help us by telling us how we learn the table of 5?" Kai asked.

"The 5 times table is so easy. It always ends with 5 or 0. When you multiply 5 by an odd number, the product ends in 5. If you multiply by an even number, the answer ends in 0," explained the lead dancer.

"But what about the digit before 5 or 0? How do we remember them quickly?" asked Nevan.

"If you are multiplying by an even number, take half of this number as the first digit. And if you are multiplying by an odd number, take half of the even number just before this odd number," she said.

"Oh, okay. So, to find 5 x 6... 6 is even. Half of 6 is 3, next comes... 0. 30," said Nevan.

"And 5 times 9 is... 9 is odd. Half of 8 is... 4, and next comes 5. 45," said Kai.

“Cool. When is the Dance Festival? Can we take one of these flyers?” Aria suddenly sounded interested in the art form.

“Why not?” Ms. Lin handed her a flyer from the pile on the nearby table.

“Can you ask your mom to check the parents’ messaging group to see which song they would prefer for your grade’s dance? Find out and let me know tomorrow,” Ms. Lin asked Aria.

“Oh, the Parents’ group! If there are 30 parents, there will be 60 song suggestions. Then there will be a big argument starting with the song, and the fight will move on to other things. It is better you decide the song without asking our parents,” said Aria, who knew how things worked in that group.

Ms. Lin nodded, indicating that she understood.

“Thank you. Bye,” the three walked off.

“Why did you take the flyer? Are you attending the Dance Fest?” Nevan asked Aria.

“No, Kai, please write the table of 5 on this,” said Aria, handing over the flyer to Kai. The three sat down on the amphitheater steps to catch their breath.

"Mr. Davidson asked us to sit, learn, and write the tables. And here we are... doing exactly the same thing. Wow!" exclaimed Kai.

5	x	1	=	5
5	x	2	=	10
5	x	3	=	15
5	x	4	=	20
5	x	5	=	25
5	x	6	=	30
5	x	7	=	35
5	x	8	=	40
5	x	9	=	45
5	x	10	=	50
5	x	11	=	55
5	x	12	=	60

Right behind the Main building was the building called 'The Annexe', which housed the labs, the school library, and the Music Room.

As they entered The Annexe, there was a long corridor leading to the library. The labs were situated on both sides of this corridor. Although the three had been to the labs once, they didn't know which lab had a microscope.

They read the boards kept outside the doors... Computer Lab, Physics Lab, Chemistry Lab...

"Hey, I have an idea. Why don't we get into the computer lab and ask the latest AI chatbot about the treasure?" asked Aria.

"Will it know?" doubted Nevan.

"Last week, I asked it where my missing green underpants were. It had no idea. Its intelligence is so artificial!" said Kai.

"Come on, let's give it a try," Aria went in, and the two followed.

Aria sat at the first computer and started typing in the chatbot, "Hi. How are you doing?"

"Hello! I'm an AI, so I don't have feelings, but I'm here and ready to help you. How can I assist you today?"

"Why are you saying all that 'Hi' and 'Hello'? Don't waste time," Kai became impatient.

"My dad says that AI and machines will take over the world soon. So, it's good to be nice to them now. I don't want to be kicked around by them in the future, you know," explained Aria.

"Where was a treasure hidden in my school during the World War?" Aria typed in.

"I don't have access to historical information specific to individual schools or events that occurred during World War I or II. Schools during wartime periods often served various purposes, such as shelters, hospitals, or areas for community support, but there isn't typically documented information about hidden treasures in schools during those times."

"See, I told you. Let's not waste any more time," said Kai.

The three ran out of the computer lab.

"Now, do we know which lab will have the microscope?" Kai asked the other two.

"Aah, here comes Dany, the tenth grader on our school bus. Let's ask him," said Aria.

Dany was coming from the Math Lab at the end of the corridor. He was the Secretary of the School Math Club for the year.

"Hi, Dany. Can you help us find which of these labs will have a microscope?" asked Aria.

"The Biology Lab has one," Dany replied.

"Thank you."

"But why do you guys want the microscope?" Dany became suspicious.

The large clock above the library entrance was ticking. Aria was not sure what to reply to Dany. In a moment of silence, all three could hear the clock ticking. Kai thought for a second and jumped in between.

"We were actually trying to learn the times tables and then..." said Kai, knowing Dany's interest in Math.

"Oh, the Times Tables. Yes, it's good to learn them at your grade. You will be much faster in solving problems of multiplication and even division. There are a lot of things in the higher grades, which will become easier for you if you know the tables well. And, of course, you will need them outside too, in the supermarket, in the mall, and yes, to calculate your pocket money," Dany took a pause.

“Yes. Do you have any easy tips to learn the table of...nine?” asked Aria, remembering the question she could not answer in class the day before.

“Nine? That’s an easy one. Listen.”

Dany signaled the three to move aside from the middle of the corridor where they were standing.

“9 x 2 begins with a number one less than 2, which is 1. And then the second number will be the number that, when added to the first, gives 9,” said Dany.

The three looked a little confused.

“Okay, look. All the numbers in the table of 9 have digits that add up to 9 itself. So, 9 x 2 = 18, where 1 + 8 = 9. 9 x 3 = 27, where 2 + 7 = 9. Got it?”

“Yes!”

Dany took a sheet of paper from the folder he had and started writing the numbers as he spoke.

“And 9 x 2 starts with 2 - 1 = 1, 9 x 3 starts with 3 - 1 = 2, 9 x 4 starts with 4 - 1 = 3, and so on. The next digit will be 9 minus the first digit. So, 9 x 3 = 2, 7...27. Then, 9 x 4 = 3, 6, and so on.”

"Wow, that's so easy," said Kai.

"Yes. And then there is a trick to use your ten fingers on your hands to check this," continued Dany.

"How's that?" Nevan asked.

"Hold your palms facing you, like this. If you want to calculate 9 x 5, turn in the fifth finger from the left. Look at the count on its left... 4 fingers, look at the count on its right... 5 fingers. So, it's 4, 5... 45."

Nevan started checking 9 x 6.

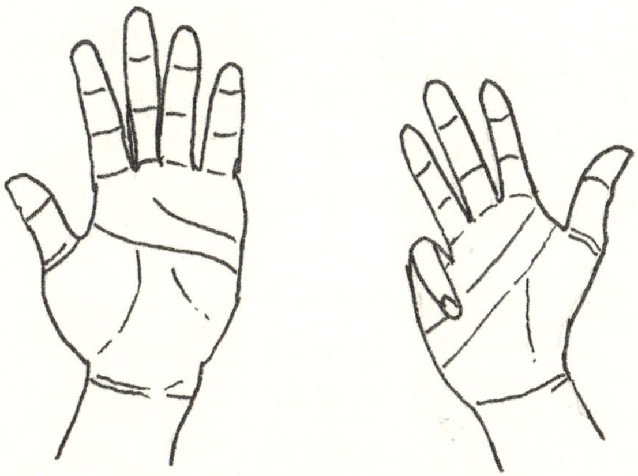

"Oh, that means when Mrs. Rodriguez asked Nine Fives yesterday, I had the answer in MY HANDS, literally. But I couldn't tell," said Aria, smiling.

"This rule works up to 9 x 10 = 90. After that, there is a slight change."

"The first digits will be two less than the multiplied number, and the last digit will be 18 minus the first digit. So, 9 x 11 will have 11 – 2 = 9 as the first digit and 18 – 9 = 9 as the second digit. 9 x 12 will be 12 – 2 = 10 followed by 18 – 10 = 8. So, 108."

"Awesome," Aria was surprised by how easy the table of nine was.

Dany handed the sheet of paper he had written on to Kai.

9 x 1 = 9
9 x 2 = 18
9 x 3 = 27
9 x 4 = 36
9 x 5 = 45
9 x 6 = 54
9 x 7 = 63
9 x 8 = 72
9 x 9 = 81
9 x 10 = 90
9 x 11 = 99
9 x 12 = 108

"There are a few more shortcuts in tables. Do you know the squares of numbers?" continued Dany.

"Yes. 3 squared is 3 x 3 = 9, 4 squared is 4 x 4 = 16...," said Nevan.

"Yes. Imagine anything in a square shape," said Dany.

Probably because lunchtime was nearing, Nevan imagined his lunchbox. Of course, he couldn't imagine it without pasta in it.

"If you imagine that square to have 3 units on one side, the square will have a total of 9 units. Like this,

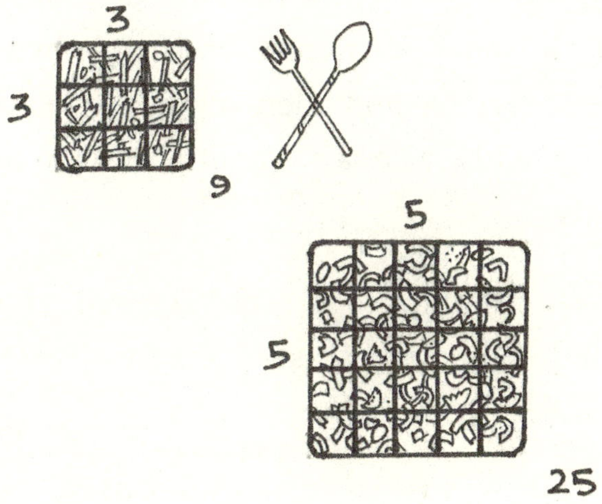

"And 5 squared is a square with 5 units on each side. Like this one," continued Dany.

"Yes, it will have 5, 10, 15, 20, 25 units in it," observed Aria.

"Wow, that's true," exclaimed Kai.

"Good. If you know the squares, you can find many tables easily. For example, 'Five sevens are?' asked Dany."

"7 is odd. So, half of six is 3, then 5...35," Kai found that using the table of 5 he learned from the dancer girl.

"Okay, you know that for the table of 5. But look, 5 and 7 are alternate numbers with 6 in between. 6 squared is 36 and then minus 1 equals 35. 5 multiplied by 7 equals 6 multiplied by 6 minus 1 equals 35."

"Aha! So, 7 multiplied by 9 is 8 squared minus 1? 64 minus 1 equals 63?" asked Nevan.

"Yes. You can also use the squares to quickly find the product of adjacent numbers. Eight nines are eight squared plus one more eight. 64 + 8 = 72. Right?" said Dany.

"Oh yeah," said Aria.

"We know that eight nines are the same as nine eights, and solving nine eights is child's play with the hand trick you showed," Nevan said.

"Cool. Yes, if you know how to quickly reverse the order of numbers in your mind, you can find the products that initially seemed difficult to you," said Dany.

"Yes, we learned that from Mr. Stewart, our school bus driver," said Aria.

"Awesome. He is a cool guy," said Dany.

"Not so cool," said Nevan. "He keeps scolding me for standing up while the bus is moving."

"Maybe he knows Newton's laws of motion, which can explain why you should not stand or move around in a moving bus. So, obey him," said Dany.

The three nodded seriously, although they had no idea about Newton's laws.

"Do you know an easy way to learn the table of 8 as well?" asked Kai.

Dany thought for a moment and said, "You know, in the long jump, it's easy to jump for the maximum length with all your efforts. But if someone asks you to jump a distance shorter than your best jump, it won't be easy. Similarly, it's easy to quickly think of a number multiplied by 10. For multiplying by 8, I used to take the number X 10 and then quickly subtract the number X 2 from it. Both X 10 and X 2 are easy to think of, aren't they?"

"Oh. So, it's like 8 x 6 = 6 x 8 = 6 x 10 – 6 x 2 = 60 – 12 = 48. Okay," Nevan did a quick check.

Kai started writing the table of 8 on the back of the sheet Dany gave.

"And 8 x 6 is actually 7 squared minus 1, which equals 49 - 1 = 48," Aria confirmed using the method for multiplying alternate numbers.

"And can we use this jumping back for 9 as well, can't we? 9 x 7 is 7 x 10 - 7, which equals 63," asked Kai while writing.

"Bingo!" said Dany. "All these tips and tricks help you find the tables initially. Once you practice with them and use them on a daily basis, you will start knowing the tables by heart. That is the objective, and then you can use them to solve more complex problems quickly."

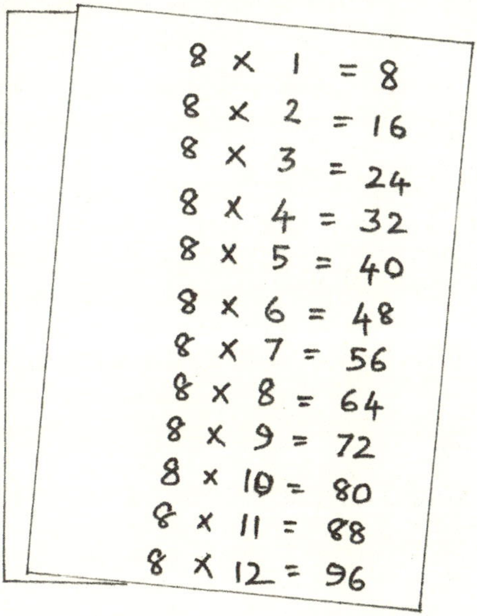

Aria looked at the clock above the entrance of the library. There were only fifteen minutes left for the free period to be over.

"Thanks, Dany. We learned a lot from you. I will join the Math Club from the next monthly session," said Aria and then signaled to Nevan and Kai to make a move.

“Yes, you are welcome. I think you, Nevan, are already a member, aren’t you?” Dany looked at Nevan.

“Yes, I love the club sessions,” said Nevan.

“See you in the next session,” said Dany as he walked away.

As he walked to the exit, Dany remembered something and turned around to ask.

“Hey, why did you want the microscope to learn tables?”

The three had already entered the Biology Lab by then.

CHAPTER 6

The fight with the class leader

Kai knew exactly where to look. He started scanning the drawers and cabinets below the microscope table. Luckily, there were no students in the lab, and the lab staff was at her desk in the other corner.

“Where can we get an amoeba to put beneath the microscope?” whispered Aria.

"Here it is," said Kai, holding a small, folded piece of paper.

"Is that an amoeba?" wondered Aria.

"Not Amoeba. The clue!" said Kai.

"Let's get out first and then check it," said Nevan.

"Of course, after 4, this one is the table of 5," Kai found out as soon as he unfolded the old piece of paper, standing outside The Annexe building.

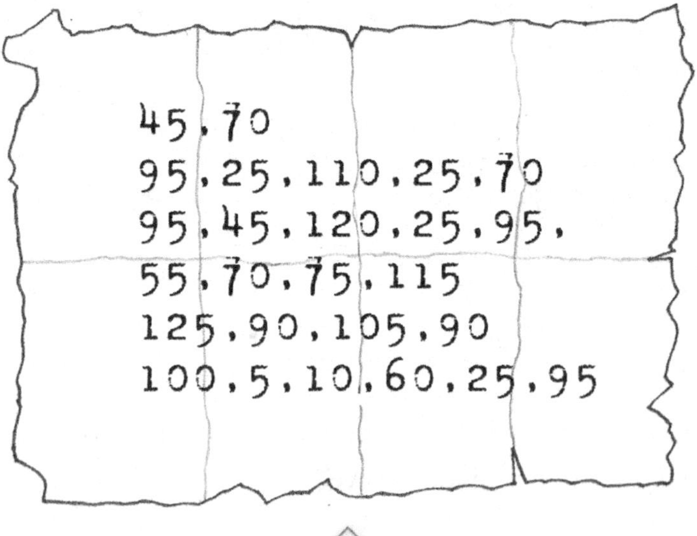

"5 is easy. The rule of the lead dancer works for multiplying with two-digit numbers as well," said Nevan.

"But there are some big numbers here," said Aria.

"See, 45 is 5 x 9 as you just noticed while talking to Dany. 70 is 50 + 20. 50 is 5 x 10 and 20 is 5 x 4. So, 10 + 4 = 14... 70 is 5 x 14," said Nevan as he wrote down the numbers one by one and Aria wrote the alphabets:

IN SEVEN FIVES, KNOW YOUR TABLES

"Oh, the 7-5 Shop, it is right there," Kai pointed to the 7-5 general store on the back side of the Main building.

"Know your tables. We know them by now," said Nevan.

"Almost," said Aria.

Nevan looked at her.

"We've learned the tables of 2, 3, 4, 5, and 9, and then an easy way for 8. What about 6 and 7?" asked Aria.

"Don't forget the reverse route technique from Mr. Stewart. Six or seven times any number is that number times six or seven!" said Nevan.

"Oh, YES!" Aria cried loudly.

"But, what about 6 x 7?" asked Kai.

"6 multiplied by 7 is 6 squared plus 6, which equals 36 + 6 = 42," answered Nevan.

"But what about 7 x 6?" asked Aria, laughing.

The three laughed and ran towards the 7-5 Shoppe.

Since the lunch break had not yet started, the shop was almost empty. The three barged in and started looking for places to search.

"Hey! What are you doing here?"

The three turned and were shocked to see Tanya, the Class Leader, standing with a fiery look.

There was a long silence of three seconds, which felt like three hours for Aria.

"Uh, hm. We came to buy candies to distribute in the class for my birthday tomorrow," said Kai.

"But where were you until now? Did you take so long in the bathroom?" Tanya was visibly upset.

"Yes, I mean no. We went to..." Nevan was not sure what to say.

"Tell me, what are you doing here?" Aria shot that question to Tanya, interrupting Nevan.

“Me? I came to get a chocolate to give to the Most Disciplined Student of the Week,” Tanya said proudly.

“Ha! Chocolate instead of discipline. You are giving it to influence someone to make your job as Class Leader easier. This is bribery. This is illegal,” alleged Aria.

“What? MDSW is a recognition forum, which is appreciated by Mrs. Rodriguez,” argued Tanya.

“Wow. Let all the criminals start calling bribery a recognition forum or whatever. The courts will send them to extra social work,” Aria raised the pitch.

“No way. Let’s go to the principal and clarify this now,” shouted Tanya, shaking slightly.

“Okay, let’s do that,” Aria was also not ready to back off.

Kai intervened as the situation was getting out of hand. “Guys, guys. If you go to the principal, she will first ask why all of us are in the 7-5 during class hours.”

"Yes, there will be no recognition or bribery forum. The whole thing will become a punishment forum, and all of us might end up getting that extra social work," added Nevan.

Tanya sighed. Aria took a deep breath.

"Listen to me, Tanya. I voted for you in the elections. I don't want you to get into trouble," Nevan tried to cool down Tanya.

"So, what? I see those who voted and those who didn't vote for me in the same way, that's my duty. At least that's what my mom told me," said Tanya.

Before Tanya could speak the last sentence, Kai had shouted, "Great, I didn't vote for you."

There was a silence that felt like the calm before a storm.

Kai quickly turned to the shopkeeper to avoid the storm. "Hey boss, I need some of this candy."

"Uh-huh," the old man was lazing in his chair a few meters behind the counter. He was in no mood to get up.

Aria was a bit annoyed. "Boss, why is the customer only King, and not Queen? What about gender equality?"

The old man turned his neck to the board and exclaimed to himself, "Oh, my gosh. Doing business has become so difficult these days."

"Sir, I need a lot of candies," said Kai, trying to avoid another fight and lure the old man to get up.

"Okay. How many dozens?" asked the shopkeeper, slowly getting up.

"Dozens? Okay, let me think."

"You mean twelve ones are twelve, twelve twos are twenty-four... like that?" asked Nevan.

"Ya. You want two dozen?"

"No, no, wait. Let me see. I need sixty candies for the class and bus together," said Kai.

"So, you need five dozen," Tanya said.

The three turned to Tanya with a face asking, "How?"

"I was just studying the table of 12, and I found an easy way to multiply a number by 12."

"What is it?" asked Nevan.

"To start, when multiplying 12 by a number, place the number itself as the first digit and its double as the second digit. For example, when calculating 12 x 3, place 3 first and then, its double, which is 6, next. Therefore, 36."

"Aha! That's easy," said Aria.

"But it changes slightly from 12 x 5," said Tanya.

"Yes, it should have been 5 followed by... 10?" asked Kai.

"Yes, just change that slightly. For instance, move the 1 in the 10 to the digit in the tens place, which changes 5 to 6. The zero of 10 remains, making it 60."

"Wow," noted Nevan.

"Continue this rule. Put the next number of the number being multiplied first and then the last digit of double of the multiplied number. So, 12 x 8 will begin with 9 and then have the last digit of double of 8, which is 6. So, 96."

"Okay," said Aria.

"Then, from 12 x 10, add 2 to the number being multiplied and continue putting the last digit of the number multiplied by 2. For 12 x 11, put 11 + 2 = 13 first and then the last digit of 11 x 2, which is 2. Hence, 13,2, that is 132," Tanya explained with a proud face.

"Wow, Tanya. You are awesome," said Kai.

"Thank you," Tanya continued to wear that proud expression.

Kai turned to the shopkeeper. "Please give me five dozen of these and the bill so that I can write down the table of 12."

"Okay. Children, please come back to the class quickly," said Tanya, walking out of the shop.

"Children? Has she now become our mom?" Aria frowned.

"She taught us the 12 times table, that's why!" observed Kai.

"Kids, it is actually not that complicated as that angry girl explained," the shopkeeper said. "7 dozens mean 7 tens and 7 twos. So, 70 and 14, 84."

"Wow. That's similar to the trick for 8 Dany told us. Here it's easier, you jump to 10 and then in the same energy jump 2 more," said Nevan.

"Yep. 12 sounds so difficult, but it's so easy," agreed Aria.

The three continued looking around for any clue while the shopkeeper packed the candies and took the bill from the computer on his table. Kai started writing the table of 12 on the bill while Nevan and Aria kept looking around, but they could not find anything. They came out of the shop dejected and stood there for a minute.

TRNGGG! The lunch break started.

12 × 1 = 12
12 × 2 = 24
12 × 3 = 36
12 × 4 = 48
12 × 5 = 60
12 × 6 = 72
12 × 7 = 84
12 × 8 = 96
12 × 9 = 108
12 × 10 = 120
12 × 11 = 132
12 × 12 = 144

Nevan looked at Kai and Aria.

“I think we should now go to our class,” said Aria.

“But we didn’t find the next clue,” said Nevan, who seemed to have forgotten about his pasta.

“Nor the treasure,” said Kai.

A few students started coming out of the school building, and some walked into the 7-5 Shoppe. A pair of twins from the eighth grade went in.

"Whenever I see these two girls walking, I feel like I'm seeing the number 11. Both the same," said Aria with a slight smile.

Kai and Nevan smiled, although they were still dejected and tired.

"You can also consider 22. Or maybe 33," said Kai.

"Those form the table of 11," said Nevan.

"That's correct. Just put the number twice. 11 x 6 = 66, 11 x 7 = 77," said Aria.

"And 11 multiplied by 11 is 110 + 11. And 11 multiplied by 12 is 11 squared plus 11. So, 121 + 11 equals 132. Same as 12 multiplied by 11," Nevan continued, but without any excitement in his voice.

"So, maybe the Seven-Eleven store near our home wanted to name themselves 77, but the owner was a clever math guy who named it Seven-Eleven instead," Aria wanted to crack a joke to lighten the mood.

Nevan smiled, but Kai didn't. His eyes opened wide as he looked at the other two. Then he hurriedly pulled out all the papers from his pocket.

"Guys, look here! The clue said Seven 'Fives' and NOT Seven 'Five'."

"Means?" asked Aria.

"Seven Fives is not the same as Seven Five," said Kai

“YES. Seven Fives is 5 x 7 = 35,” Nevan was also excited now.

“So, the clue says we need to be in 35?” Aria was also excited now.

“But where is 35?” asked Nevan.

There was a 10-second silence, which felt like just one second for the three whose minds were racing.

“The room number of classrooms!” said Kai.

“Oh yes, every room in the school has a number as well. So, which one is Room Number 35?” Nevan’s voice was rising.

“It is our class. The Math class from which we sneaked out!” said Aria.

“I have seen the number above the door. It’s our class,” Aria repeated, looking at Kai and Nevan.

“Let’s go.”

CHAPTER 7

Oh, my gosh!

The class was in its usual chaos during the lunch break. The three walked around the class and checked inside the lockers, behind the screen, and all the corners of the room. They could not find anything that could lead them to the treasure. They sat down in their seats. There was enough time left to have lunch, but the three were in no mood to open their lunch boxes. Not even Nevan!

“We are in room number 35 and we know the tables. Now what?” asked Nevan.

“Do we really know the tables? Let’s write the ones we have not written so far,” said Kai, quickly checking all the papers he had.

“We need to write for 6, 7, and 11,” said Kai.

“Nevan, write 6. Kai, do 7. I’ll take 11, the most difficult one,” said Aria, smiling.

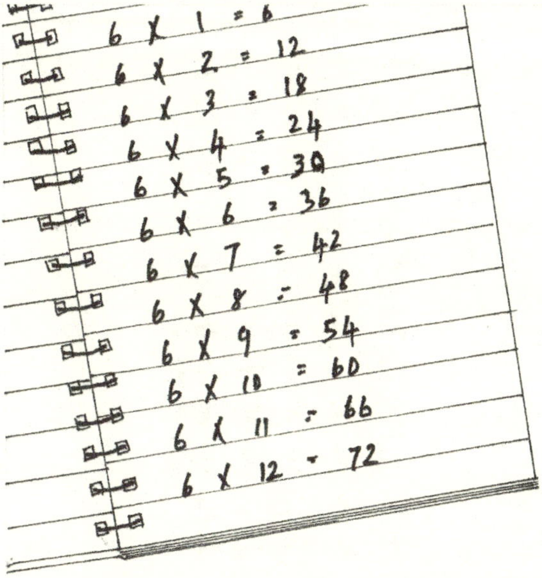
6 X 1 = 6
6 X 2 = 12
6 X 3 = 18
6 X 4 = 24
6 X 5 = 30
6 X 6 = 36
6 X 7 = 42
6 X 8 = 48
6 X 9 = 54
6 X 10 = 60
6 X 11 = 66
6 X 12 = 72

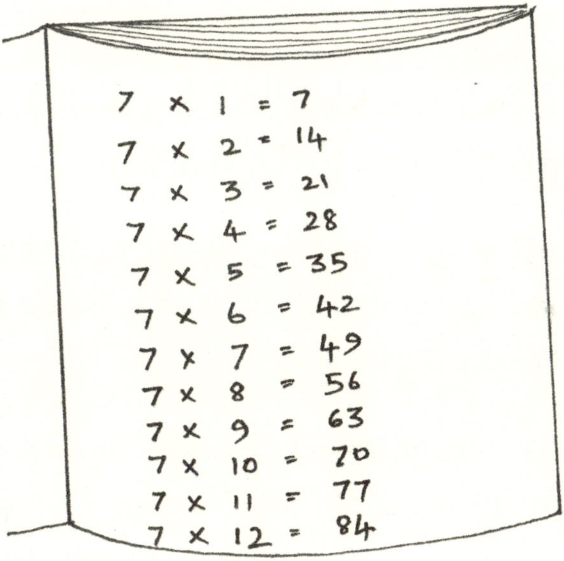
7 x 1 = 7
7 x 2 = 14
7 x 3 = 21
7 x 4 = 28
7 x 5 = 35
7 x 6 = 42
7 x 7 = 49
7 x 8 = 56
7 x 9 = 63
7 x 10 = 70
7 x 11 = 77
7 x 12 = 84

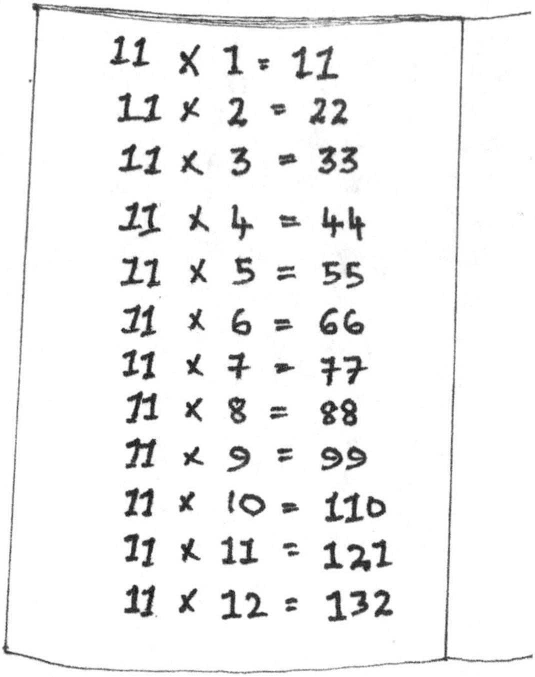

"We know our tables," said Nevan in a loud, disappointed voice.

"Yes, old man, I also know my table. It's blue in color, and my lunch box is kept on it," said a voice from behind.

The three turned around. Of course, it was Snoopy Sasha, having her lunch and now enjoying a good laugh.

"It's okay, Nevan. We all know about our chairs and tables. No need to shout," said Sasha, continuing to chew her food.

The three turned back.

"She doesn't even understand which tables we are talking about," Nevan said softly to Kai.

"Do we really know our tables?" asked Aria to both of them.

"What?" wondered Nevan.

Kai started looking at his table, first at its top blue surface, then at the sides. Aria bent down beside the table.

Nevan looked at Aria and then at Kai. Kai was kneeling on the floor, looking at the bottom surface of the table. He appeared frozen, with his mouth open in astonishment.

"OH MY GOSH." The scream was loud enough for the whole class to hear despite the chaos. It was Aria, down on her knees beside the table.

She slowly got up, smiling artificially at those looking at her.

"Sorry. Sorry," she said and sat in her seat.

"Have you gone crazy?" Nevan whispered to Aria. He turned to Kai and noticed that his mouth was still open.

Kai moved closer to Nevan. "There is a piece of paper stuck to the bottom of the table."

Nevan's heart almost stopped.

"There's one here too," whispered Aria.

Nevan slowly got up from his seat, glanced under his table, and stood back up.

"Yes. It's here too."

Kai went down and slowly took the piece of paper that was stuck with some sort of glue.

"I have never looked under any table in my entire life," Nevan said to Aria.

"Neither have I... after I spotted a cockroach under a restaurant table once," said Aria.

Kai passed the paper to Nevan.

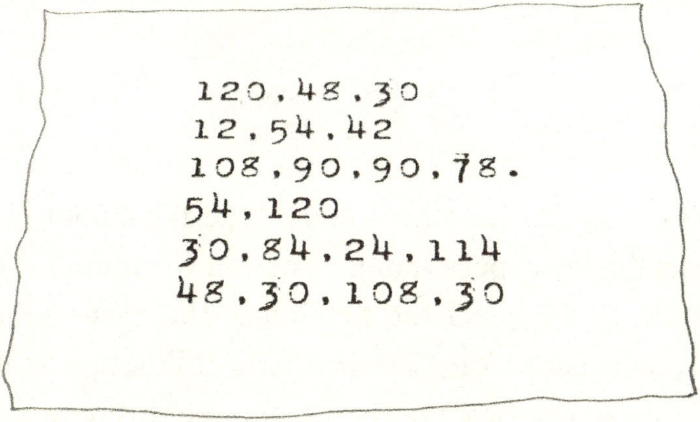

Aria passed the paper below her table, and it had the same numbers.

"Yes, it's the 6 times table. I just wrote it," confirmed Nevan, and started writing the alphabet numbers on the same paper.

Nevan started calculating in his mind, "120 is 12 x 10, and 12 is 6 x 2. So, 6 x 2 x 10, which is 6 x 20, is 120, and the first number is 20. 48 is 6 x 8, so the next is 8. 30 is 6 x 5, so 5..."

Once done, he quickly passed it on to Aria, who identified the alphabets by the numbers and wrote the message

THE BIG ROOM. IT ENDS HERE.

TRRRNNGGGGG!

Everyone in the school knew 'The Big Room.' It was the Principal's room, right in the center of the Main Building on the first floor, the same floor as their classroom. Usually, only children caught doing some grave mischief got to see this room.

The three had to rush to the school bus after the day's class. On the way down, instead of the staircase near their class, they took the one in front of The Big Room. They caught a glimpse of the room when the door opened. It was the Principal, Mrs. Woods, walking out. The three turned their heads away, looked down, and rushed to the bus.

Once inside the bus, Aria wanted to talk, "So, it is in The Big..."

Kai signaled Aria to be silent and to talk later.

Aria turned and checked the seat behind, expecting to see Sasha with her mouth filled with snacks. To her surprise, Sasha was not there, but her regular bus mate was there.

"Where's Snoop...err...Sasha?" asked Aria.

"She was picked up by her mom after class today. She had an appointment with the doctor to clean her ears of earwax," said Sasha's friend.

"Aah," exclaimed Aria, then turned to Nevan and whispered, "Of course, her ears have to be clean and wide open."

Kai got off one stop early again.

“So, the treasure is in the Principal’s room. How are we going to search for it?” asked Aria.

“I have no idea. She will be in her room throughout the day,” said Nevan.

“Mrs. Woods goes out for a walk in the corridors after her lunch during the break time,” said Kai.

“So, we will have our lunch, go near The Big Room, wait for her to leave, and then sneak in,” Aria concluded.

“We will have fifteen minutes to find the treasure, which is the time she normally takes for the walk,” said Kai.

“I think it’s better if one of us stays outside and gives a signal if she is coming back,” suggested Aria.

“I will do that,” said Nevan, who was already a bit nervous.

“Okay, you will give a whistle if you see her coming. I have read that in a Fantabulous Five Adventures story,” said Aria.

"Oh, I don't know how to whistle," said Nevan.

"Okay. I'll stay outside," Aria volunteered.

"But how will you whistle into the Big Room from outside, without anyone else hearing it?" asked Kai.

"Nevan, don't you have the walkie-talkie set that you received from our neighbor Henry as a birthday gift last month?" remembered Aria.

"Oh yes! But Henry himself borrowed it from me the next day to play."

"What? Just go and take it from him today. I'll carry one, and you carry the other one into the Big Room tomorrow," said Aria.

Nevan nodded.

"Guys, guys! What will we do with the treasure?" Kai asked suddenly.

"We already decided, right? We will eat pizza from the cafeteria every day," said Nevan.

"Ha! It's a treasure, not pocket money. You will have to come to the school even after you graduate if you have to spend all that money only on pizzas," said Aria.

"I meant...," Kai wanted to speak, but Aria continued talking.

"Let us donate the money to the school for building a swimming pool. Maybe we can ask for a swimming period every day, since we are giving so much money."

"Good idea. It should be named after us – like 'The Talented Three Pool' or something," replied Nevan.

"Let's also donate a new bus, which will be only for the three of us," added Aria.

"Yes, we can sleep a little more and start from home a little later every day if the bus is just for us," said Nevan.

"Guys, guys, I was asking about how we will carry out the treasure from the room when we find it there," Kai intervened finally.

The three thought for a while.

"Let's empty out the books and carry our bags into the Big Room," suggested Aria.

"Okay, let's carry whatever we can in the bags," agreed Kai. "So, we are finding the treasure tomorrow. See you guys."

Kai walked off.

CHAPTER 8

1942... how it all began

The three had a similar set of thoughts, tension, and anxiety during the rest of the day.

How will we find the treasure in the principal's room? Will the principal or anyone else catch us trying to get the treasure? Are we stealing the treasure that belongs to some other family? If someone from that family exists today, will they sue us? Will the school agree to name the swimming pool and a bus in our name?

Nevan handed a walkie-talkie to Aria as soon as they met in the morning. Kai simply smiled and sat beside them on the bus. There was no discussion, but the tension was evident on their faces.

As soon as the break started, they gobbled up their lunch. The three kept all their books on the seats and took the empty bags. They walked out of the class towards The Big Room without looking at anyone's face. Their hearts were pounding.

As they neared the room, Mrs. Woods suddenly burst out and started walking in the corridor in the opposite direction they were coming from. They looked at each other.

Nevan and Kai walked into the Big Room. It was indeed very big, as the name suggested.

"Nevan, check the cabinets over there. I'll check these cupboards," said Kai.

Aria was looking toward the end of the corridor where Mrs. Woods turned right. The corridors were filled with students during the break, and noise levels were high. She had one hand on the walkie-talkie in her pocket.

"Nothing here," said Nevan.

"Check the drawers of the table," said Kai.

Aria was still looking at the end of the corridor. She suddenly felt the noise level behind her decrease. She turned around and saw Mrs. Woods walking towards her from the corridor on the opposite side. Mrs. Woods had descended to the Ground Floor and then ascended from the other end of the main building.

Aria quickly turned to the other side and picked up the walkie-talkie, "She's here, she's here."

Nevan looked at Kai. Kai ran over from the cupboard to Nevan near the table.

"Stop her, Aria. I mean, distract her. Talk to her about something. We are still checking," said Kai.

Nevan looked under Mrs. Woods' table to see if there were any 'under-the-table' clues. "Why does she have such a big table? She has no books to study or notes to write."

"What will I talk to...," mumbled Aria.

"Hi, Miss. That is a nice gadget to carry to school."

Aria's heart stopped as she heard this behind her. She turned around to see Mrs. Woods right in front of her.

"But unfortunately, the school rules do not allow any electronic devices," continued Mrs. Woods.

She checked Aria's name on her ID card.

"Come, Aria, let's talk about this," said Mrs. Woods, walking towards the Big Room.

Aria was standing frozen, not knowing what to do.

She ran behind Mrs. Woods into the room.

Nevan and Kai were sitting on the guest chairs in front of Mrs. Woods' table, peeping underneath.

"Good afternoon, boys. What brings you here?" asked Mrs. Woods as she walked towards her chair.

Kai almost fell off the chair out of shock. Nevan pulled the walkie-talkie down to hide it. Aria walked behind Mrs. Woods and sat on the empty chair.

"Yes, tell me," said Mrs. Woods.

Aria gained the strength to speak. "Mrs. Woods, there is a treasure in your room."

Mrs. Woods kept looking at Aria for three seconds. These three seconds felt like three seconds itself to Aria.

"Give me a second," said Mrs. Woods.

She took her phone and started dialing.

"Who is she calling? Police? Parents?" thought Aria, who had started sweating.

"Good morning, Mrs. R. Do you have a class now? Which class? Okay, can you please come to my room?" Mrs. Woods hung up the phone.

"So, tell me your names, children," Mrs. Woods asked Nevan and Kai.

They replied.

"May I come in?"

It was Mrs. Rodriguez, the math teacher.

"Is Mrs. Woods planning to share the treasure with Mrs. Rodriguez?" Kai was trying to figure out what was happening.

Mrs. Rodriguez took a seat and turned to the three.

"Hey, my children. How are you?" she asked.

"We are good. Thank you," said Aria.

"Mrs. R, they seem to have found a treasure in the school," Mrs. Woods told Mrs. Rodriguez.

"Interesting. What happened, children?" Mrs. Rodriguez asked the three.

The three together briefly narrated the incidents from the time they saw the old piece of paper pinned onto the soft board in the class.

"So, why didn't you search for the treasure in my room?" asked Mrs. Woods.

There was silence for a second.

"Err...we thought that the treasure belongs to either the family that hid it or the school where it was kept for so long. Hence, we thought you would be the best person to manage it," Nevan managed to reply.

"I'm impressed," said Mrs. Woods and turned to Mrs. Rodriguez. "Can you please explain about this TREASURE?"

The three turned to Mrs. Rodriguez.

"Ok, Aria, Nevan, Kai... the entire treasure hunt was planned by Mrs. Woods and me for the students in your grade. We strategically placed the clues in all the locations where you discovered them, and then we displayed the first clue in your classroom. The goal was to assess the curiosity levels of our students and provide a distinctive way to learn the multiplication tables."

"You mean, YOU did all this?" Nevan's tone was raised.

"Unfortunately, yes. But fortunately, you will find a treasure," said Mrs. Rodriguez, turning to the principal.

"Yes, each of you will get a set of twenty-five chart-topping children's books. It is a gift from the school for the curiosity and persistence you showed. From what you explained, it appears you cracked the whole hunt in about one hour. This shows your willingness to learn, your math and language skills, logical abilities, and above all, the spirit to work together as a team," said Mrs. Woods.

"Thank you, Mrs. Woods," said Aria. Her sweaty face had now transformed into a smiling one.

Nevan heaved a big sigh of relief.

"But those paper pieces looked really old and were from a typewriter," Kai was a bit disappointed still.

"Oh yes. It took me some effort to find an old paper and make it look older. I knew about the World War rumor that circulates in the school. And the typewriter, it's a wonderful font named

1942 available on my computer," explained Mrs. Rodriguez.

"And, didn't anyone else from our class find the treasure?" asked Kai.

"No,"

"But it's below everyone's table, right?" asked Nevan.

"Yes. But someone just finding the message below the table may not understand the secret multiplication table code used unless they have gone through the other clues and learned the tables as you children did!" said Mrs. Rodriguez.

"Oh, okay. So, is the treasure hunt over now?" asked Kai.

"Not yet. We want you to keep this undercover for a few more days. We will now put the clue up in the other division class of your grade, and keep the other clues in their places again, and keep it open for one more week. We will then give out the gifts, I mean THE TREASURE, in the Open Assembly," said Mrs. Rodriguez.

"That will be awesome," said Nevan.

"Mrs. Rodriguez, we received assistance from Mr. Stewart, Mr. Watson, Ms. Lins, her lead dancer, the 7-5 shopkeeper, and Dany, the Math Club Secretary, to learn the tables and follow the treasure," said Nevan.

"And Tanya too... our Class Leader," added Aria.

"Wow. We will also announce their names in the Assembly to give them the due credit," said Mrs. Woods.

"But finally, it was you three who showed the energy to overcome challenges and made our plan a success. Kudos to you," said Mrs. Rodriguez, shaking hands with each of them.

"Now, you can go back to your class with Mrs. Rodriguez. Her first period is in your class itself."

The three came out smiling at each other.

"Don't talk about this to anyone, okay?" reminded Mrs. Rodriguez before entering their class.

The three nodded and walked to their seats, looking around proudly.

Jay was still looking out through the window.

And they lived happily ever after... Hey, wait! Did you see the table of ten? No!

But don't worry. Sasha had written it down since the three missed out on writing it. Oh, no! Was she snooping on them all the while?

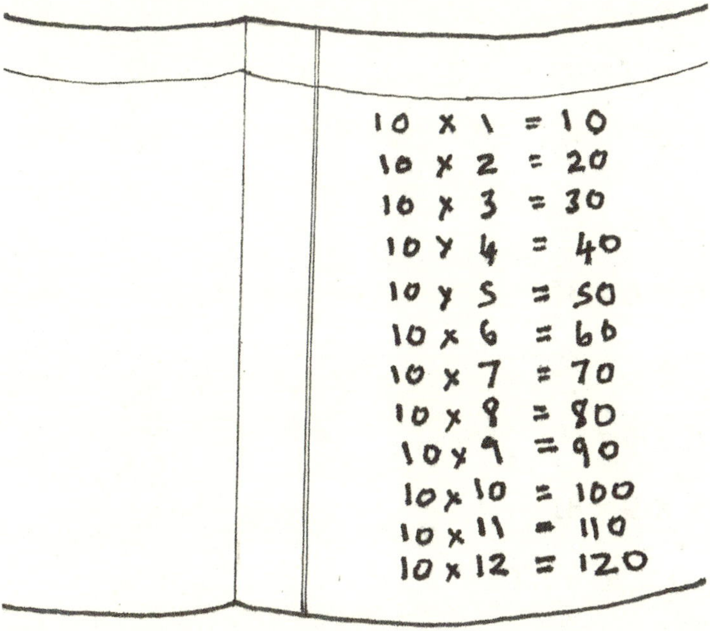

Square of all numbers

1 X 1 = 1

2 X 2 = 4

3 X 3 = 9

4 X 4 = 16

5 X 5 = 25

6 X 6 = 36

7 X 7 = 49

8 X 8 = 64

9 X 9 = 81

10 X 10 = 100

11 X 11 = 121

12 X 12 = 144

Times Table Grid

Times Tables

x	1	2	3	4	5	6	7	8	9	10	11	12
1	1	2	3	4	5	6	7	8	9	10	11	12
2	2	4	6	8	10	12	14	16	18	20	22	24
3	3	6	9	12	15	18	21	24	27	30	33	36
4	4	8	12	16	20	24	28	32	36	40	44	48
5	5	10	15	20	25	30	35	40	45	50	55	60
6	6	12	18	24	30	36	42	48	54	60	66	72
7	7	14	21	28	35	42	49	56	63	70	77	84
8	8	16	24	32	40	48	56	64	72	80	88	96
9	9	18	27	36	45	54	63	72	81	90	99	108
10	10	20	30	40	50	60	70	80	90	100	110	120
11	11	22	33	44	55	66	77	88	99	110	121	132
12	12	24	36	48	60	72	84	96	108	120	132	144

Times Tables Games

Game 1: Dice Tables Challenge

Get two classic six-faced dice, and off you go!

Multiplayer: Player 1 throws the two dice together. The sum of the numbers rolled (a random number from 1 to 12) becomes the First Number for this round of the Tables Challenge. Next, Player 2 throws the dice together. The sum of the two numbers rolled becomes the Second Number, and finding the correct product of the First Number and Second Number is the Tables Challenge for the round. The player who calls out the right answer first (by saying First Number X Second Number = Answer), after the dice are rolled for the Second Number, gets 10 points. In the next round, Player 3 throws the dice first, and so on. You can play for any number of rounds – 12, 24, 36, or 48.

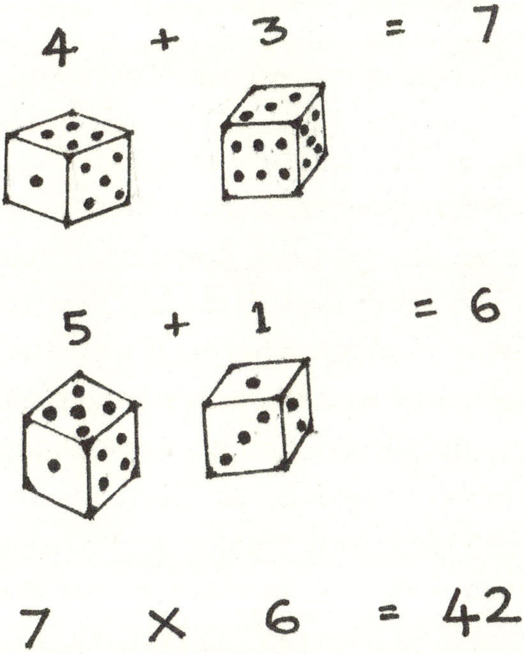

Single player: Set and start a timer for 144 seconds (2 minutes, 24 seconds). Roll the dice, as above, quickly to find the First Number and Second Number. Find the Product and write down First Number X Second Number as soon as possible. Continue rolling the dice and writing down the Product. After the timer goes off, check the Products written and count the number of correct answers, which will be your score for the round. Try to improve your score in the next round.

Game 2: **Deal the Tables**

Grab, beg, borrow or steal a deck of playing cards

Multiplayer: In a pack of cards, A is considered as number 1, Q as 11, K as 12, and all number cards as per their number. Keep aside J and Joker cards. In the first round, deal 6 cards each to each player. Player 1 picks up her cards first. The player can select any two cards in her hand, pair them together, and display it to everyone saying 'First Card Number X Second Card Number = Product'. She has to keep the remaining cards also in pairs by saying the Product as above. If any product is wrong, other players can call out, and the player has to say again with the correct answer. The time taken from the player taking her cards to finishing the display of all cards noted down. Each player takes their hand and does the above. The player with the minimum time wins the round. You can play for any number of rounds – 12, 24, 36, or 48. After each 12 rounds, the number of cards dealt to each player is increased by 2 – from 6 to 8, to 10, and so on. The times taken are added at the end, and the player with the lowest total time is declared the winner.

Single Player: The rounds are played as described above by a single player, aiming to reduce the time taken to finish each round.

NOW THAT THE TREASURE IS TAKEN, PICK *YOUR GIFT!*

Can you think of any other tips and tricks for learning times tables or multiplication?

Which is your favorite scene/incident in this book?

Can you click a picture of you playing the Challenge games yourself or with friends?

Send me any one or more of the above on email at cv.jayagovind@gmail.com to win an action-packed downloadable **FUN ACTIVITY BOOKLET** with puzzles, coloring and more based on your favorite book - Treasure in the Multiplication Maze.

Now, for the **BIG BONANZA**...

Send me the details of humorous or awkward incidents in your school life and stand a chance to get it featured in my next book, with credits duly acknowledged!

(Yes of course, I'm getting my work done by you. Thanks, in advance. But hey, don't you think it'll be a bragging opportunity for you?? You're welcome.)

There's something for the TEACHERS too...straight from the desk of Mrs. R!

Teachers and educators, send an email at cv.jayagovind@gmail.com with your review of the book to get a FREE **Discussion Guide for Teachers**. The guide will help you utilize this book - Treasure in the Multiplication Maze - to help your students learn the times tables.

The **FREE Downloadable Discussion Guide for Teachers** will include:

- ✓ How to discuss the book content in class
- ✓ Exciting Math Activity sheets
- ✓ Times tables games to play in the class
- ✓ & much more

And PARENTS, how can I forget you!

In return for all the chores you get the kids to do, you need to follow me on your favorite social media (only if you are on social media, else enjoy life). Don't worry, I won't spam your feed, I'm too lazy to post every day. But whenever I get good ideas, tips or thoughts on parenting and learning, I vow to share them.

@jayagovind

facebook.com/cv.jayagovind

jayagovindcv

Acknowledgment

Thank you, Siddhi and Sreepad for sharing all the stories and thoughts from school, allowing me to imagine the present-day school life.

Thank you, Lekha, for motivating me to write and being patient all the time.

Thank you, Aadhya, Aju, Sumod, Indira, and Chechi for giving your time, feedback, and ideas.

Thank you, Navsangeet, Brijesh, Shrikesh, Vinay, Amit, Rajit, and the entire White Falcon team for the wonderful work in editing, proofreading, designing, and publishing to make this book a reality.

About the Author-cum-Illustrator

1500 years after 'zero' was invented in India, Jayagovind was born in the same land. This multi-generational connection to the number stuck with him from childhood as he boasted of his talent to answer the multiplication of any number with zero in a jiffy. However, his teachers were unimpressed, so he set out on the adventure of learning the remaining tables the hard way - with a Times Tables book.

His adventures continued as he went on to graduate from the College of Engineering, Trivandrum, and pursue post-graduation from the Indian Institute of Management Calcutta. After working for 15 years with a large bank, he co-founded Window Seat (windowseat.ai), a children's book and game subscription service, to facilitate child learning through fun.

And then... he was reminded of his childhood 'times' when he overheard his kids' online math classes. He helped the kids break the times tables down into smaller chunks, adding some easy-to-memorize tricks. Knowing that stories are a great medium to convey concepts to children, he set out to create this book, to help many more children realize that all tables are as easy as the table of zero (well, almost).

Made in United States
Orlando, FL
23 June 2025

62332366R00080